Bing Brings a Bug

By Carmel Reilly

This is Bing.

Bing has red wings
and a red chest.

Bing has chicks in the nest.

Bing will bring bugs
for them.

Bing clings to a stick.

He sings and sings.

But here is Steff!

"This is **my** home, Steff!" sings Bing. "Go away!"

"I can sit here!" sings Steff.

Bing flaps his big wings.

Zing!

He pecks Steff!

Bing wins.

Bing gets a sip at a pond.

But what is **that** thing?

It's a bug!

Will the bug sting Bing?

No, Bing can get the bug.

Bing brings the bug
to his chicks.

The chicks scoff the bug!

CHECKING FOR MEANING

1. What sounds does Bing make when he sings? *(Literal)*

2. What does Bing do at the pond? *(Literal)*

3. How do you think Steff was feeling in the story? *(Inferential)*

EXTENDING VOCABULARY

wings	Look at the word *wings*. What is the base of the word? How does adding *s* to the end of the word change the meaning? Find another word in the book where *s* has been added to make it mean more than one.
It's	Look at the word *It's*. What is the punctuation mark in this word called? Why is it there?
scoff	What does the word *scoff* mean in the story? What is another word with a similar meaning? What other meaning can scoff have?

MOVING BEYOND THE TEXT

1. What do birds eat besides bugs?

2. What do birds make nests out of?

3. What other animals can fly?

4. Why do you think Bing didn't want Steff near his nest?

SPEED SOUNDS

| at | an | ap | et | og | ug |

| ell | ack | ash | ing |

PRACTICE WORDS

Bing

wings

bring

clings

sings

Ting

Ping

Zing

thing

sting

brings